I0079408

HOW TO SMOKE FISH

INCLUDING BRINE CURING
DRY SALTING HOME CANNING

BY

H. T. LUDGATE

Copyright © 2013 Read Books Ltd.
This book is copyright and may not be
reproduced or copied in any way without
the express permission of the publisher in writing

British Library Cataloguing-in-Publication Data
A catalogue record for this book is available from the
British Library

CONTENTS

Preserving and Canning Food:
Meat Curing

Food preservation has permeated every culture, at nearly every moment in history. To survive in an often hostile and confusing world, ancient man was forced to harness nature. In cold climates he froze foods on the ice, and in tropical areas, he dried them in the sun. Today, methods of preserving food commonly involve preventing the growth of bacteria, fungi (such as yeasts), and other micro-organisms, as well as retarding the oxidation of fats that cause rancidity. The earliest curing consisted of nothing more than dehydration; early cultures utilised salt to help dessicate foods, and this was a well-known technique almost everywhere on the globe. Food curing dates back to ancient times, both in the form of smoked meat and as salt-cured meat. The Plains Indians hung their meat at the top of their teepees to increase the amount of smoke and air coming into contact with the food. Drying, essentially reduces the water content sufficiently to prevent bacterial growth, and salt (or sometimes sugar can be used) draws the moisture from the meat via a process of osmosis. In the 1800s, and before, chefs and lay-people alike experimented with different sources of salt (rock salt, sea salt, spiced salt etc.) and it was discovered that certain types of salt gave meat a red colour, instead of the usual, and somewhat unappetising grey. The active ingredients in this type of salt would have been either nitrates or nitrites, and they also helped inhibit the growth of Clostridium botulinum; a toxic bacteria often found in old meats. In the new age of consumerism, this technique was soon picked up by butchers and store-keepers alike to appeal an increasingly prosperous population. This salt, often coloured pink to differentiate it from table salt, is now used in cured meat production on a massive scale. Sea salt added to raw ham to make Prosciutto, has became one of the best known, and most expensive exports of central and northern Italy. Today, we do not simply cure and preserve out of necessity, but because we enjoy it.

FOREWORD

THERE is real fun and satisfaction in smoking or preserving fish. On your very first attempt you are almost sure to get fair results—here's why: The smoking process is such that wide variations are permissable in all the steps involved.

A little salt, more or less, a couple of hours smoking, more or less, and a selection from any of a dozen kinds of smoking woods—all may make for slightly different flavor, color, or texture. The point, however, is that the finished fish will be delicious. So, get in there and try your luck—soon.

SMOKE YOUR OWN FISH

HERE is a brand new experience for most sportsmen—smoking your own fish. You are in for a real treat, for even the lowly carp imparts a flavor that makes you value every morsel. Take it from a fisherman who has discovered for himself this old but little practiced art that you can get fine results the first try and your smoked fish will be the envy of the gang.

Digressing for just a moment from the "How To Do It," let me tell you of an incident about smoking fish up in the north woods. The catches were unusually good, so we set up a small rig for smoking, made from an old packing case. Boy, what flavor! What feeling of accomplishment to get in production and preserve for future treats our daily catches!

The top of this most satisfying experience came one day when we tied our boat at the dock of an old guide, where we tanked up with spring water, and almost apologetically offered some of our smoked Northern Pike. A few days later we were all but embraced by the woodsman—"Never," said he, "in all the years I have been up here have I tasted anything so delicious! How do you do it"?

In the years that followed, the many friends who have tasted our smoked delicacies invariably wanted to know how it was done, listened wide eyed to the simple secrets we had gathered from many sources, and went away treasuring their new found formula. And so here you have in this simple unpretentious form, never before printed, our findings on fish smoking, condensed secrets derived from many sources. While the methods used are basically similar to those of the commercial fisherman, this pamphlet is written for the sportsman or villager who wishes to preserve his own catches. It makes no difference how few fish you have—don't put off trying your hand at fish smoking.

HOW SMOKING WORKS Fish flesh is an extremely perishable food. Almost immediately after death, the muscle substances begin to undergo changes through the action of digestive juices, the so-called enzymes which are present in the muscles themselves. These changes, called autolysis or self-digestion, produce an unpleasant flavor and odor. (In the ripening of meat a certain degree of autolysis is desirable.) Autolysis, which is accelerated by increasing temperature, is soon overtaken by the action of bacteria, which invariably gain access to the fish muscle, mainly from the surface slime of the fish, the gills, and the guts, where they occur in immense numbers. For example, one grain of slime from the skin of a cod or salmon may contain as many as 47,000,000 bacteria when the fish is out of water 12 to 24 hours.

Bacterial decomposition of the fish muscles takes place at a much faster rate than the initial autolytic changes. It is mainly in order to retard the spoiling action of bacteria that methods such as salting, drying, canning, freezing, and smoking are used. Smoke serves as a chemical disinfectant; that is, a substance which, if used in sufficient concentration and for sufficient length of time, will not only inhibit bacterial growth and action but will kill the bacteria. Smoking is primarily a preserving treatment, but to the lover of rare treats, it is an unequaled flavoring process as well.

SALT PLUS SMOKE DOES JOB The smoke alone does not do the job, but is aided by the action of a strong salt brine. Salt inhibits bacterial growth. Marine life that may thrive in one or two per cent salt is, with few exceptions, inhibited by five per cent salt. Salt draws water from the fish and this drying action further tends to retard action.

Wood smoke contains a number of aldehydes, especially formaldehyde, as well as acetic acid. Formaldehyde has not only been proved to be present in smoke, but also in a variety of smoked products, such as herring, raw smoked ham, bacon, and similar products. Formaldehyde has long been known to exert a peculiar effect upon gelatin, which, if treated with it, will not melt on subsequent heating, even after prolonged boiling. Smoke also has the same action upon gelatin. If fish muscle is treated with either smoke or formaldehyde, its tensil strength is increased, which means that it can not be torn apart as easily as can fresh fish. This is due to the hardening of the connective tissue. The action is similar to that of the hardening of gelatin under the same treatment and reminds us that gelatin is closely related to animal connective tissue.

The bacteria killing action of smoke continues after the smoking, due to certain substances deposited on the fish during the process. Bacteria whose resistance has been lowered by the brine treatment are now made ineffective by the smoke and its residues.

THE 1-2-3-4 OF FISH SMOKING The whole process consists simply of

1. Immersing fish in a certain strength of brine.

2. Air drying to rid the flesh of excessive moisture.

3. Smoking in a hard wood smoke for a specified time.

4. Taking care of the finished product, wrapping, etc.

MAKING THE SMOKEHOUSE There are as many ways of making a smokehouse as there are of killing a cat. The notion seems to prevail that there is some mysteriously exact requirement in every detail of the construction to produce just the right results. This is all wrong. When you understand what your smokehouse is supposed to do, then you can go ahead and make it out of anything that is handy.

You simply want an enclosed box, barrel, or frame structure that will permit smoke to be admitted at the bottom, and small holes at the top to let a certain amount of the smoke out so as to keep the smoke in circulation, away from the fire. Some means is needed of holding the fish by the tails or head so that the smoke may circulate freely around the fish—usually this is nothing more than a stick with nails driven into it, and the stick is held horizontally by cross cleats.

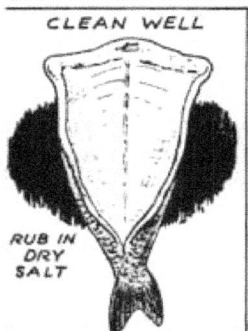

VARIOUS SMOKEHOUSE ARRANGEMENTS Following are several arrangements for a smokehouse—each works equally well. Your selection of the type to make will depend upon the permanency of your smoking operations, the number of fish you are likely to be handling at a time and the material you may have available to make the smokehouse. It isn't a bad idea to make your first attempt at smoking with a simple rig, then as you get into it, make one with refinements that will best suit your needs.

SMOKEHOUSE FROM A BARREL, Fig. 1, Right. Here is about the simplest form of "smokehouse"—an ordinary barrel. You will be amazed at the fine quality of smoked fish that can be turned out from such a simple rig.

Knock the ends out and place barrel over one end of a shallow pit, connected by a shallow flue to the fire pit about ten feet away. The flue can be made with an old piece of stove pipe, a few drain tile, or simply by cutting away the sod (about one foot wide by one foot deep), then covering the shallow trench thus made with a piece of tin, wood slats or anything that is handy. Place sod over the tin to give a cleaned up appearance to the rig, and also to retain the smoke and to hold down the draft. If possible it is best to make a dog-leg bend in the flue to hold down the direct draft, to prevent sparks, etc., from endangering the barrel, and to prevent overheating.

A flat top or barrel end is required to close the top rather loosely and a piece of burlap may be thrown over the top to further retard the smoke from the barrel.

HERE'S THE SIMPLEST SMOKEHOUSE

Fig. 1—Smokehouse From a Barrel

Wire hooks hung down over the sides of the barrel support sticks to which are nailed the fish to be smoked—see cross sectional drawing, Fig. 1. If a piece of wire screen is available, place it underneath the barrel—it will catch any fish that may come off the nails. The wire will also help spread the smoke more evenly. An odd piece of sheet iron will be required to place over the fire pit to smother the fire for suitable smoking.

HANDY SIZE RIG FOR AVERAGE FISHERMAN, FIG. 2. No attempt has been made to give dimensions for these may be varied within long limits and still do an excellent job.

If you have an old packing box anywhere near the proportions of this sketch—use it. A hinged cover is handy but not essential as the cover can be tacked in place. The sticks which hold the fish rest on cleats so that the sticks may be taken out of the box and loaded with fish, then simply laid across the cleats when ready to smoke.

The flue may be made of stove pipe, although for permanence some drain tile are fine. If you can find slightly sloping ground, then let the fire pit be lower than the smoke box which will allow smoke and heat to circulate. If possible, have a bend in the pipe to cut down the direct draft and passing of larger sparks. The holes, about five one inch holes, may be cut in the top or on the sides just below the top. It is well to have plugs or corks for these holes so that the amount of "draw" in the system can be regulated. Sod placed around the bottom of the box will hold everything rigid.

The fire pit is simply a hollowed out place that doesn't need to be more than a foot or so in diameter. If a reclining slice is made in the slanting ground (lower right corner Fig. 1) in shaping the fire pit, you can see how handy it will then be to place the tin over the pit to smother the fire for smoking. Sod placed around the edges of the tin will give you any degree of draft desired.

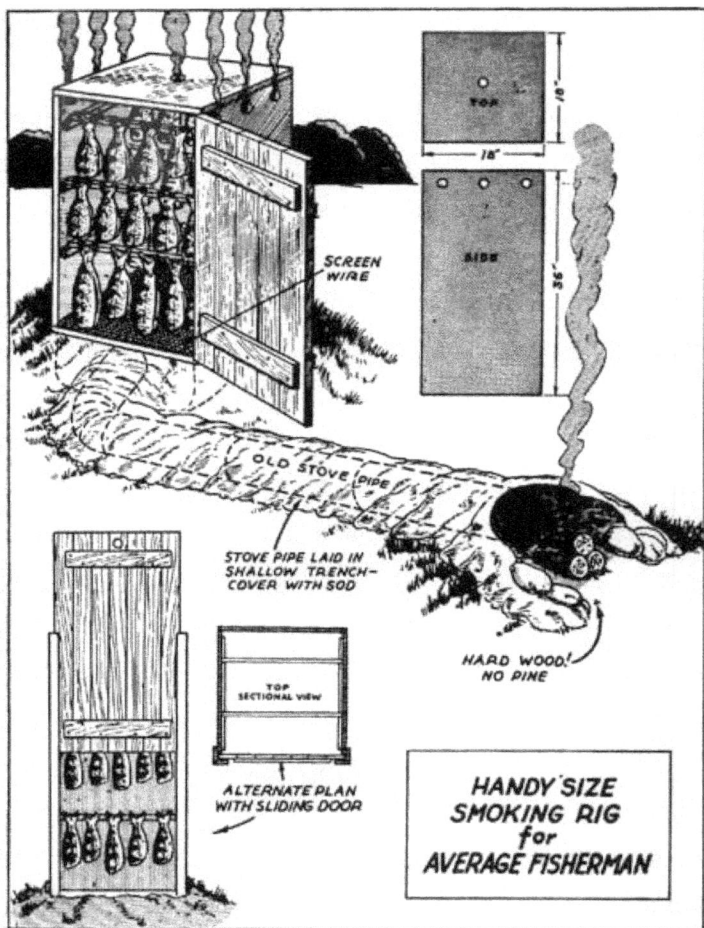

Fig. 2—Popular Size For Yard or Camp

14

LARGER SMOKEHOUSE—FIG. 3 (RIGHT) Essentially this smokehouse operates exactly as the simplest barrel type, but it has certain refinements and if you have a permanent location in the back yard or at the cottage, you will find this a fine house to build.

Instead of holes there is a top vent with a slide that is adjustable.

A smoke spreader is made at the bottom from a can punched full of holes. This tends to eliminate hot spots in the box and to smoke the whole batch evenly. Sometimes a sliding tray is used to hold the fish but this is not so good because the wire mesh leaves marks on the fish and the smoke circulation is not as good as around a suspended fish. There are other variations of the smoke spreader: an inverted large lard pail, slats across the flue outlet, a wooden box with holes,—use whatever is handiest.

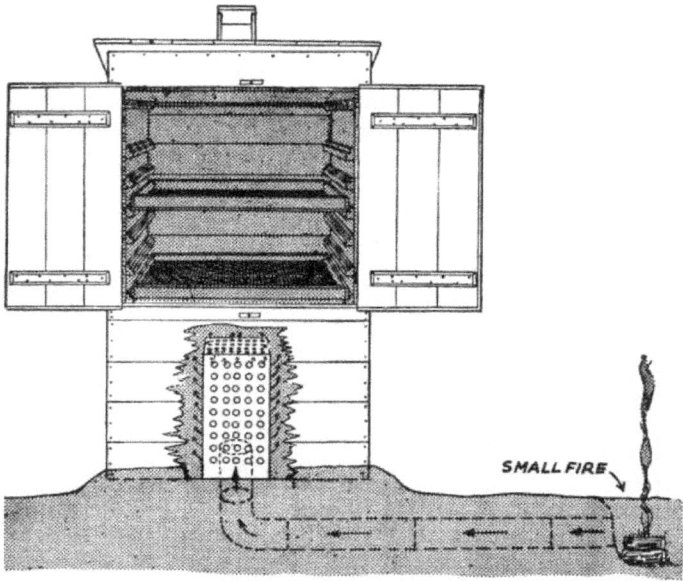

SMALL FIRE

Fig. 3—A Larger Smokehouse
Courtesy U. S. Bureau of Fisheries

In this type the fire is removed from the smokehouse, the smoke is spread out by passing through a tin box which has many holes in it. A ventilator at the top is adjustable and controls the draft and amount of smoke and heat. This is a permanent smokehouse and is recommended where the demands for production at any one time will not be large. Because of its design features a smokehouse of this type would lend itself to cooler smoking, which is required in prolonged smoking for hard curing, for example, two days or more.

PERMANENT SMOKEHOUSE, FIG. 4, RIGHT Many

fishermen will find need for a good substantial smokehouse that will handle good size catches, possibly on a commercial scale.

The smokehouse in Fig. 2 is possibly the best all around size for the average fisherman who goes out on occasional week ends or vacation trips. The larger smokehouse in Fig. 3 is fine where the rig does not have to be moved far and greater capacity is desired. But for permanence, and generous capacity you'll find this design (Fig. 4 Right) in good favor. While the dimensions are given, they may be changed to suit the material at hand.

TAKE FIRE PRECAUTIONS The essential difference between this house and the others is that the fire is built on the ground, within the smokehouse, thus no flue or fire pit is required. There is possibly better regulation of draft for the principle air vent on the door may be controlled with less guesswork. The big drawback to making this smokehouse is that the sheet iron for the sides and top is not always readily at hand. In this construction, and in fact any smokehouse, avoid an arrangement that will place the fish too near the top of the box. It is considerably hotter near the top and will cause uneven processing of the fish.

Caution. A commercial fisherman, friend of the author, built a smokehouse of this type years ago but failed to use sheet iron. In just a few ungarded moments, the house caught on fire with a total loss of smokehouse and the fish. In any kind of smoking there is the ever present danger of fire. Take every precaution.

So much for the smokehouse construction—you are now ready to run a batch through—a real experience and worth all the effort.

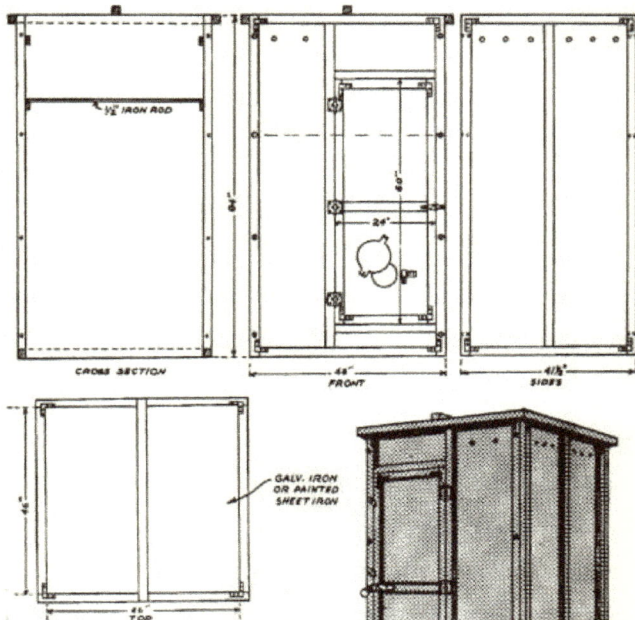

CROSS SECTION

FRONT

SIDES

GALV. IRON
OR PAINTED
SHEET IRON

TOP

PERMANENT SMOKEHOUSE
COURTESY U. S. BUREAU OF FISHERIES.
FEATURES: FIRE IS ON GROUND INSIDE
SMOKEHOUSE. ADJUSTABLE DRAFT
ON THE DOOR. SIX 1" HOLES ON
EACH SIDE AT TOP. A SLIDING
DEVICE GIVES VARIABLE OPENING
OF HOLES; OR THEY MAY BE CORKED.
FOUR ¼" BOLTS AT EACH VERTICAL
EDGE HOLD HOUSE TOGETHER.

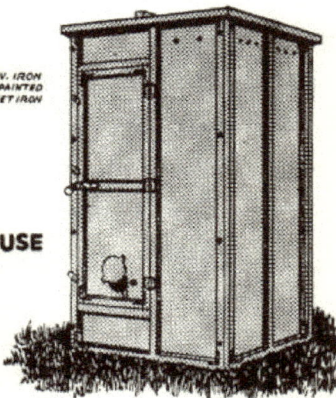

Fig. 4—A Good Rig For Larger Catches

CONVERT YOUR OUTDOOR OVEN TO A SMOKEHOUSE

If you already have a nice outdoor oven in your back yard, or at your cottage, then you can make it serve double duty. Simply follow these easy to handle details illustrated on the right.

There is one precaution that must be taken in using this type of rig—avoid overheating. In this rig the fire is almost directly beneath the fish and it is very easy to let it get out of hand. It will materially lessen the danger of overheating if you will use only small pieces—naturally the greater the size of the glowing, smouldering chunk, the greater the heat given off. It is much better to run your rig too cool than too hot. Remember, if it is too hot to comfortably leave your finger in one of the holes for half a minute, it is too hot for continued smoking for any length of time.

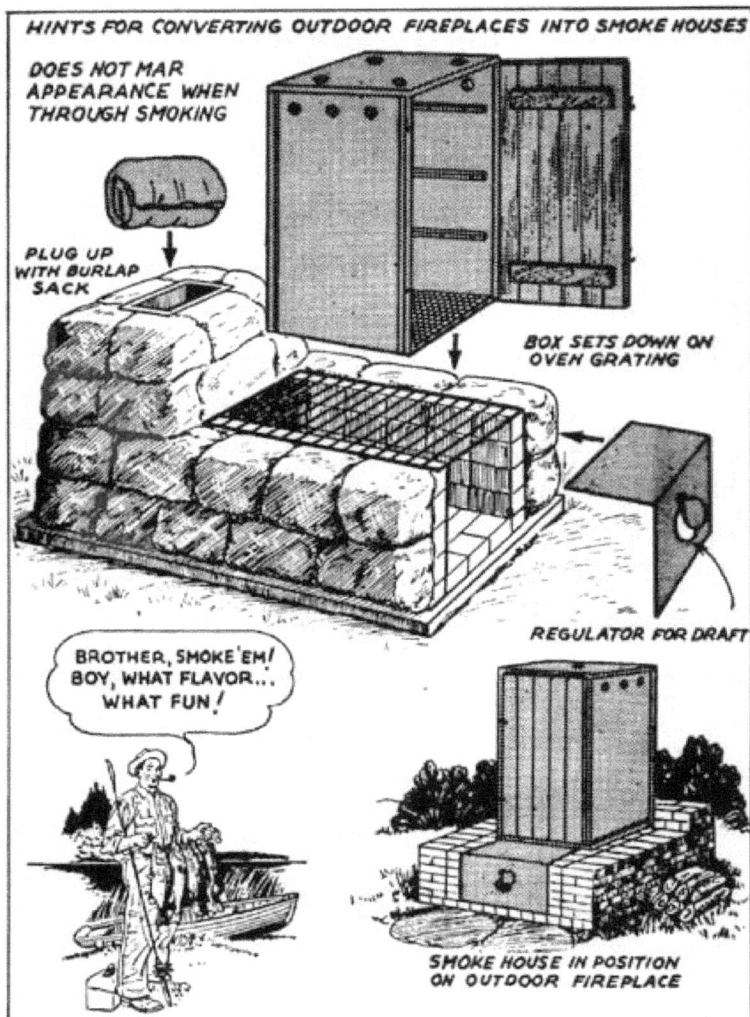

SIMPLE SECRETS OF
FISH SMOKING

*Wide Variation in Method is Permissable—Learn To
Smoke To Your Own Taste.*

In this short treatise it would be impossible to take up every specie of edible fish and tell what particular special treatment should be given it for best smoking. Rather the aim shall be to give you the steps and details that are essential for practically all kinds of fish smoking and minor variations can be made to suit the needs at hand. This is intended as a guide and not an infallible recipe. To smoke fish successfully, you must experiment and use your intelligence, altering the method according to your own taste (amount of smoke flavor or saltiness), the variety of fish, and weather.

FOR BEST RESULTS SMOKE ONLY FRESH FISH. The idea somehow prevails that fish in about any condition will come out all right in the smoker. This is absolutely wrong. You must have freshly caught fish for best results. As explained previously, fish flesh deteriorates fast and no amount of smoking is going to restore a bad condition. Treat your fish for smoking as carefully as you would fish for immediate consumption and you'll be repaid well for the trouble. If the fish are to be transported any distance in hot weather, before starting the smoking operations, then ice them down so as to keep in best possible shape. Another alternative is to clean the fish and hold them in brine until you are ready for smoking.

Practically any edible fish may be successfully smoked. Differences in firmness of flesh, fat, etc., will of course cause the finished product to differ.

PREPARING FOR SALTING In preparation for salting, the fish is first split along the belly from the head to the vent and the entrails removed. The head may be left on; however, the writer feels that most sportsmen will prefer severing the head which will permit smoke coming in contact with the thicker, meatier portions behind the head. Scales should be left on, although with carp and bowfin the fish should be fleeced, i.e., the scales removed, along with the thin underlying skin, with a sharp knife. Wash thoroughly. Fish having a dark abdominal lining should be scrubbed with a stiff brush until the lining is removed.

If the fish are small, no further treatment is necessary before placing them in the brine. If they are large, weighing two pounds or more, they should be split down the back from the inside, severing the ribs close to the backbone, the cut being sufficiently deep so that the fish will lie flat. Extra large fish may be cut into two or more lengths and the large body pieces split as just described. This method of preparing the large fish permits the salt to penetrate more easily and to insure a more evenly smoked product.

SALTING—VERY IMPORTANT There is considerable variation in method with different smokers and here again experiment will show the degree of salting that will best suit your taste. Here are two common methods, of which the first is widely used and probably safest:

1. Wash fish thoroughly in clean water. Rub dry salt over fish, then leave in brine over night. This brine is made by adding salt to water until it will just float a potato. Water should be clean—if in doubt about water, boil, let cool and add salt. Do not put fish in hot brine.

   For milder curing, when fish are not to be kept long, three or four hours in above brine is enough.

   Note: A satisfactory brine by weight is: one pound of common barrel salt to each gallon of water.

   While the fish are in the brine they should be inside and if possible covered over in some manner.

2. Make a cleaning brine by adding two cups of salt to four gallons of water. Leave fish in this brine 30 minutes to soak out blood diffused through fish. Take out, rinse, and remove any traces of blood or offal. Drain a few minutes, then drop each fish singly in a shallow box of fine salt,

"dredging" it about, then picking it up with as much salt as will cling to it, and packing fish in even layers in a tub or box. Leave this way from one to three hours, depending on weather, size of fish, fatness, and length of time for which preservation is desired. Rinse and remove any particles of dirt or salt.

DRYING BEFORE SMOKING Before placing in the smokehouse, the fish having been rinsed of all salt and slime, are hung out in the open air to dry for a few hours. If the day is clear and dry with a breeze blowing, the drying will take place in fine shape and leave a desirable thin film on the surface which, in turn, makes for nice appearance upon smoking. If the day is not dry, it is best to hang your fish in the smokehouse with a fire in the pit, and the door open to drive off excess moisture. If the fish were smoked without first drying, you would have an excess of moisture in the smokehouse and the meat would become steamed and softened before it had a chance to cure. Some smokers use chicken wire for drying racks and recommend keeping fish out of direct rays of the sun. For ease of handling, however, there is nothing wrong with hanging your fish on the sticks which will support them in the smokehouse so that as soon as the drying is completed the sticks, loaded with fish, may be transferred directly to the smokehouse where they are supported across the wooden cleats as shown in Fig. 2.

NAIL

HOOK
PIERCES
FLESH

TWO WAYS OF HOLDING FISH

Fig. 5

SUPPORTING FISH IN SMOKEHOUSE. A good, quick method is to simply drive a small nail, about a 3 or 4d, through the fishes tail, or just ahead of the tail. Other methods are:— passing a rod through heads, under gill covers; tying chunks of large fish with string; or passing an S hook through fish and over the cross rail as show in Fig. 5. The important thing is to so support the fish so that they do not touch, and that the box will not be crowded, and finally that the fish will not fall off. **WOOD TO USE IN SMOKING** Any dry wood, except pine, may be used in smoking fish. Hard woods are preferred. Corn cobs are satisfactory. Green wood or damp wood of any kind is objectionable because the moisture driven out with the smoke makes the fish soggy. Pine wood imparts a resinous flavor to the fish, making it very unpalatable. Dry, seasoned maple, including dry bark, birch, oak, and hickory, are choice woods. In southern states use scrub oak, live oak, hickory, sweet bay, river mangrove, palmetto roots, button wood or coconut husks. Orange wood gives a very pleasing flavor; cypress, too, is good. Apple wood is excellent.

The fire should be small but steady. Cut three chunks about a foot and a half long and about the thickness of a man's arm (Fig. 6). Start the fire by making a pile of chips with your axe or knife and after it is going briskly, place the three chunks on the fire together. Where the chunks touch will develop into a hot spot and will get the pieces going thoroughly enough that they will continue to smoulder or "burn" for a long time when the sheet iron cover has been placed over the pit to hold down the draft. It is a good idea to start the fire for a half hour or so before putting fish in the smokehouse. You will have to attend to your fire occasionally, turning the pieces of wood, If you have trouble holding your fire, occasionally add a few dry chips and fan the embers with your hat.

STACK CHUNKS IN THIS WAY

DRY CHIPS HERE TO START

Fig. 6

TWO KINDS OF SMOKING—HOT SMOKING, AND COLD SMOKING There are two distinct methods of smoking—one is a hot smoke which cooks the fish at the same time it is cured; the other is a cold smoke that cures only, and the fish must be cooked before using.

Hot smoking is similar to barbecuing the fish, it takes from three to six hours to do, may be eaten at once, and the keeping quality is from a few days to a month or more, depending upon the amount of smoking. The writer, however, has successfully kept hot smoked perch for over a year. There are special treatments for long keeping of hot smoked fish and these will be dealt with later. For your first attempts at smoking the hot smoke method is recommended because it takes less time, the food is so delicious, and because the method is adaptable to almost any kind of fish.

In the cold smoking method the temperature is kept below 90 degrees and the smoking is continued for two days or more.

The length of time for smoking varies so greatly with various smokers that one is at a loss to recommend a uniform standard. The following, however, is a "middle of the road" method for hot smoking.

Simply start with a fairly brisk fire in the pit, then smother it down with chips or sawdust and cover over the pit with the tin. Keep a low, gently smoking fire, without blaze, so that smoke oozes steadily out of the smokehouse cracks and ports. If anything it is better to keep the rig working toward the cool side for it is so easy to let the smokehouse get too hot. Place your finger in one of the port holes and if it can not be kept there without real discomfort, you have too much heat. After four or five hours of uniform, moderate smoking, finish off with from one to two hours of hot smoking by stirring the fire, and opening up somewhat the draft by cracking the tin over the pit to let in more air. Avoid letting the temperature go over 150 degrees.

During the first part of the smoking never let the fire blaze up. If it should do so, smother it with sawdust, dried bark, or by turning the chunks over on themselves.

The fish will take on a glossy brown color. This color deepens upon exposure to air. Well dried fish will color more readily during smoking than will wet fish. There are harmless coloring substances frequently used to enhance the appearance.

CARE OF SMOKED FISH The question in your mind upon completing a batch will be: how long will they keep? One can hardly answer that question for so much depends upon the salting, the temperature, size of fish, the weather, and conditions under which they are stored.

The most common way of keeping smoked fish for day to day consumption is simply to wrap each fish in waxed or parchment paper, pack in a wooden box (cheese box, oblong type is fine) in a cool dry place. Avoid letting the smoked fish come in direct contact with ice; also avoid storage in a wet cold. Regular electric refrigeration is fine. While smoked fish have excellent keeping qualities, nevertheless they should be treated as perishable food, especially during hot weather. Sprinkling over with dry salt is thought by some oldtimers to forestall molding. Another practice is to dip the fish in paraffin. The wax is removed with hot water when ready to prepare for eating.

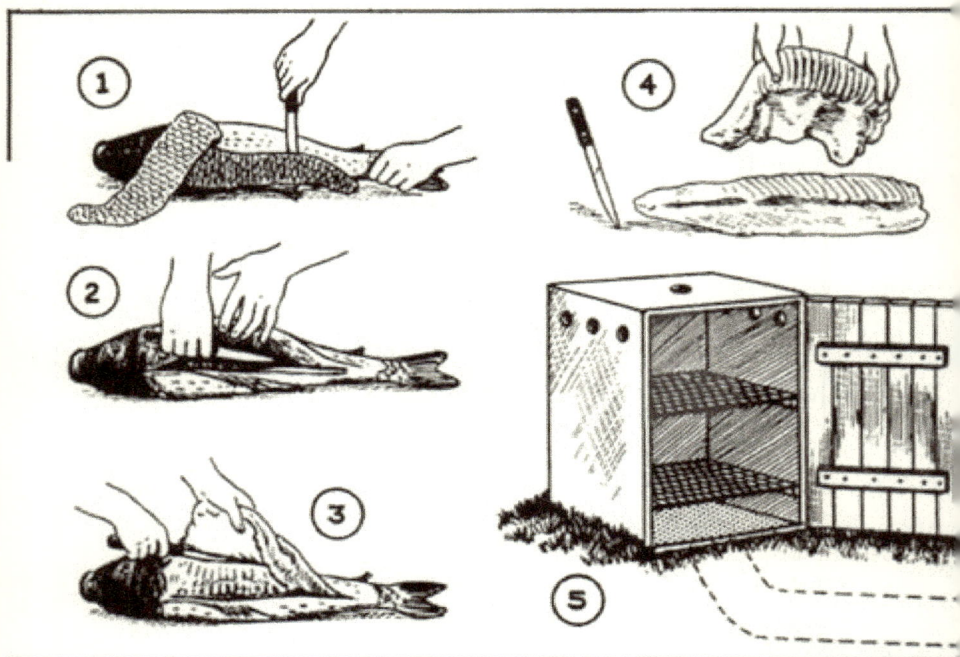

SPECIAL INSTRUCTIONS ON CARP

Use a sharp knife with a stiff, narrow blade about six inches long. Then hold the fish by the tail and slice under the scale by moving the knife in a sawing motion toward the head. See 1, in sketch above. There will be about three strips of scales on each side. This removes the scales and dark skin and leaves a clean white skin.

Next, cut down the back on either side of the dorsal fin, from head to tail, until the knife hits the bony ribs. No. 2, above.

Then cut away side steaks (No. 3) from the ribs, leaving the ribs, skeleton and internal organs with body of fish.

Score the fillets with cuts one quarter inch apart. Make a brine that will float a potato, dredge fillet in dry salt and soak in brine three hours. Make screen wire racks for smokehouse as shown in No. 5 above, lay fillets out and let dry two or three hours in breezy spot with door open. Apply moderate heat to aid drying if necessary. Close door and smoke for four to six hours. Smaller fish take less time.

Note: The above method of filleting is also recommended for preparation of carp for pan frying, especially if fish is large.

DUTCH METHOD OF KEEPING Here is an old Dutch method of treating hot smoked fish which will keep them almost indefinitely. After smoking, cut the flesh up into figures the length of a No. 2 can or pint glass jar. Skin and pack into can or jar. Then add vegetable oil (cottonseed or olive oil) until the spaces between the pieces of fish are filled and there is a layer of oil up to within an eighth of an inch from the top. Seal the can or jars and store in a cool place such as an ice box, until used. As this product is not sterilized, the can or jars should be thoroughly scalded before use. In some cases the oil is filled hot and the containers sealed immediately.

RECIPES FOR SMOKED FISH

THE HOT smoked method of smoking fish which we have largely featured in this manual does not require further cooking of the fish. The beautifully browned meat removes readily from the bones with the fingers—every last morsel is delicious eating. While for most sportsmen this will be the rarest kind of treat, to eat 'em just as they come from the smokehouse, there are, nevertheless, other methods of preparation for the table which are popularly used.

If the above mentioned "barbecued" or hot-smoked fish are to be served, the skin should be removed before coming to the table. If desired, various condiments may be used, such as pepper, catsup, relishes, onions, etc., depending upon the variety of fish and the tastes of the family. Actually, however, much of the sportsman's treasured product will be eaten "on location." Incidentally, a perfect boat lunch is three or four small smokies, plenty of crackers, and lots of water, pop, or whatever your fancy prefers for "whistle" wetting.

SMOKED FISH IN MILK

3 pounds smoked fish

1 cup whole milk or cream

3 tablespoons butter or good cooking oil

Pepper—salt, if needed

If the fish have been heavily salted before smoking, freshen one hour or more before cooking. Drain, dry and place skin side down, on a greased baking pan or skillet. Pour over the milk, adding butter and pepper and cook slowly in oven, or over slow fire from 8 to 12 minutes. Remove to platter, and pour the liquid about the fish. Garnish with parsley.

SMOKED FISH SOUFFLE

2 eggs, yolks and whites beaten separately

2 cups cooked rice

1 1/2 cups milk

1 cup cold cooked smoked fish flakes

2 tablespoons fat Salt, pepper, paprika

Beat egg yolks until thick and lemon colored. Add fish flakes, milk, rice, butter, and seasonings. Blend. Fold in carefully the stiff beaten egg whites. Pour into a greased baking dish, which, set in a pan of hot water and bake three-quarters of an hour at 350° F. Serve with or without a tasty fish sauce.

SMOKED FISH CROQUETTES

2 eggs. Use 1 in croquette mixture; use 1 in which to dip croquette when crumbing

1 clove garlic mashed and rubbed over the mixing bowl if

desired.

2 cups of fish flakes

1 cup of mashed potatoes, either hot or cold

1 1/2 teaspoons salt

1/8 teaspoon pepper Bread crumbs

Combine potatoes, salt, pepper, fish flakes and eggs, well-beaten. Mix thoroughly and form into croquettes. Roll in fine bread crumbs, then in beaten egg to which water has been added, or thinned canned milk, drain and roll in bread crumbs again. Fry in deep hot cooking oil or fat, at 39° F., until nicely browned. Drain and serve hot.

BAKED SMOKED FISH Two (2) cold smoked fish, or the amount needed by the family for one or more meals. Freshen one hour or more before cooking. (See directions above.) Remove any foreign particles, and dry. Place in a greased baking pan, flesh side up. Sprinkle well with any good cooking oil. Sprinkle with finely diced onion and carrot. Cover with milk. Bake from 20 minutes to one hour according to thickness of flesh and length of time fish have been smoked. Baste from time to time as milk evaporates. Remove to platter. Garnish with parsley. Serve hot.

CREAMED SMOKED FISH

1 1/2 cups cooked flaked fish

1 cup milk

1 cup fish stock

1 tablespoons flour

4 tablespoons fat or oil

1 teaspoon Worcestershire

Sauce

Salt, pepper

Make a medium white sauce of flour, fat, salt, pepper, liquid, and stir smooth. Add fish flakes and heat through. Variations of this may be had by adding eggs, carrots, and peas, parsley, etc.

SMOKED FISH FLAKES
SCALLOPED WITH POTATOE

1 pint cold flaked fish

4 tablespoons oil

4 tablespoons flour

2 teaspoons lemon juice

1 cup milk

1 cup smoked fish stock

2 cups cold potatoes

1 teaspoon tobasco sauce Pepper

Make a smooth cream sauce of oil, fat, liquid, add seasonings nad blend well. Place a layer of potatoes in greased casserole, then one of fish, one of cream sauce. Repeat until ingredients are used. Top with sauce. Bake until nicely browned.

PRESERVING FISH IN BRINE

EXTENSIVELY DONE All along the coast of the United States a small local business is carried on in pickling fish for use during the winter in the homes of fishermen and their neighbors. Among the species thus prepared are bluefish, squeteagues or sea trout, channel bass, croakers, perch, sheepshead, Spanish mackerel, striped bass, black bass, hog-fish, etc. The method will also apply to inland fishes of practically all types.

SIMPLE BUT EFFECTIVE There is no uniform method of pickling, the fish being dressed, salted and packed according to the fancies and convenience of the curers, and the product rarely goes on the general market. In general, the fish are dressed by removing the head and guts, and are split down the back or sometimes the belly, so as to lie out flat. They are next washed and soaked until the blood is removed and then covered with salt and placed in barrels, first a sprinkling of salt and then a layer of fish, and so on until the barrel is filled, and then pour in brine to fill interstices.

HERE'S HOW IN DETAIL The following, from an economic circular by H. F. Moore: "Preserving Fish For Domestic Use," goes into more detail.

Large fish having soft fins, small scales, and thin skin should be scaled but not skinned. Remove the head, split down the belly to the vent, and remove the viscera. Make a cut on each side of the backbone inside of the body cavity, cut the bone in two as far back as it can be reached, and remove the cut-off portion, then make a deep cut along one side of the backbone for the remainder of its length and remove the tail. If the fish are too large to go into the container, cut them to the proper length.

Slender fish, such as mackerel, whiting, large herring, etc., should be split down the back to one side of the backbone for the entire length, the belly walls not being cut. The backbone need not be removed. Smaller fish of the same character need not be split but should be carefully eviscerated. Coarse-scaled, thick-skinned, spiny finned fishes like black bass, perch, etc., should be skinned, and unless large and thick-meated they need not be split.

Having dressed and thoroughly washed the fish in water containing a little salt, taking particular care to remove the blood near the backbone, cure them as follows:

Place a layer of coarse salt on the bottom of a tight keg, barrel, or other suitable vessel, and on this spread a layer of fish, one deep, sprinkle salt thickly over these, add another layer of fish, and repeat until the barrel is full or the supply of fish is exhausted.

FIRST STAGE IS TEN DAYS The salt and moisture from the fish will make a strong brine in which the fish should be left for a week or 10 days. At the end of that time remove the fish, thoroughly wash them, repack in the barrel, and cover with a freshly made brine strong enough to float a fresh egg.

ONE WEEK FOR THE SECOND BRINE After a week the above brine should be drawn off and the barrel filled with a saturated brine, that is, one in which a little undissolved salt will remain on the bottom of the vessel, after the solution has been subjected to prolonged stirring. Do not reuse the old brine.

The barrel or keg should then be headed and stored in a cellar or the coolest place available. If there should be a leakage which may be discovered by the sound made when the barrel is struck with a stick at various heights, it should be made good by adding strong brine through a bunghole. If the receptacle can not be filled at once, the fish may be preserved by placing on top of them a cover made of a barrel head or of pieces of wood cleated together to fit the container and weighted with a clean stone or other heavy article which will not be affected by the salt. The success of the operation will depend on using fresh fish, exercising care in the salting and the proper mixing of the brine, and on keeping the barrel tight and the fish covered with strong brine.

Note: Many fishermen who may be interested in attempting the above method may be stopped for want of the right container to store the fish. Bear in mind that when a barrel is used, as is customary, the head is coopered on tight, however, this is by no means an air tight seal in the same sense as in canning. Therefore if you can find a large earthen ware crock such as is frequently used for storing eggs in water glass, this may be made to serve the purpose simply by making a wooden cover that will fit rather snug INSIDE the crock, then weight this board or cover down with a clean stone. The idea being to keep the fish immersed or "dunked" under the brine. It would be a good idea then to place another flat cover over the crock which would keep the contents free from any contamination. Would advise against using a metalic container for holding brine salted fish any length of time, such as is required in the above method.

PRESERVING FISH BY DRYING

A COMBINATION OF SALTING AND DRYING. This method is a combination of salting and drying and may be usd for small lots of fish at home or even may be done commercially.

The fish should be absolutely fresh. They should be bled when they are caught as blood decomposes more easily than flesh. Fish should not be left under direct rays of the sun in an open boat.

Mullett and Spanish mackerel are among the best fish for dry-salting, however, many other varieties may be successfully cured such as grouper, sheepshead, alewives or river herring, spot, croaker, and drum, and many others. There is no reason why any good, fresh caught fish can not be cured by this method if directions are carefully followed.

PREPARATION The fish should be split along the back, just above the backbone. They must lay flat in a single piece, leaving in the backbone. When the knife is drawn toward the tail it must not go clear through the skin. After cleaning and removing all viscera the fish should be rinsed and dropped in a tub of light salt brine (two pounds of salt to five gallons of water) and left to soak for 30 minutes. This helps remove blood and slime.

Score with a knife under the backbone and then longitudinally through the flesh and on the other side. This admits salt and aids drying. After the fish have soaked 30 minutes take them out, making sure that each one is properly cleaned. Drain for 15 minutes. If not drained the excess moisture requires more salt.

Use a "dairy fine" ground mined salt. Ordinary sea salt is more apt to cause reddening. Coarse salt is not as good as a fine salt. Pour the salt into a shallow box about two feet square. Dredge each fish in this salt, rolling it about two or three times and rubbing salt into the slashes. Pick it up with as much salt as will stick to it. Scatter a thin layer of salt on the bottom of the tub or box for salting. Then lay in the fish in an even layer, flesh side up. Be sure that no two pieces of fish touch without salt between. Scatter a little salt on top. Continue this until all the fish are in salt.

WEIGHT THE TOP The top layer should be weighted down, to keep the fish under the surface of any brine that is formed. The top layer should also be packed skin side up. Use about one part of salt to three of the fish, by weight.

THE SALTING PLACE The salting shed should be light, open, airy, and cool as possible. The fish will have absorbed enough salt for curing purposes in about 16 hours. Mackerel should be in salt about 48 hours. At the end of this time take the fish out of the salt and scrub them in a brine of the same strength as used in cleaning, to remove all excess salt and dirt. No traces of salt should be visible on the surface. After draining 15 to 20 minutes, the fish are ready for the drying racks. These are frames of wood, covered with chicken wire and standing on legs three or four feet high.

The drying racks should be placed on dry ground, preferably covered with gravel. Oxidation or rusting sets in immediately if drying is carried on under the direct rays of the sun. But if fish are kept shaded in a breezy location they will dry well with a clear color. For this reason drying is best done in the shade under a roof without walls, so located that as much of a current of air as possible will pass over the fish. The fish are laid out skin side down but are turned three or four times the first day.

PROTECT AT NIGHT The fish are gathered up and placed under shelter at night to prevent spoilage through dampness. If left spread out in the open at night, they will sour and mold. The time required for drying depends on weather conditions during the drying period, and on the size of the fish being cured. The exact time must be determined by the person curing the fish. For mullet it should average four days; Spanish mackerel, five days. The more the fish are dried, the less danger there will be of reddening or rusting. When the surface lboks dry and hard and if the thumb can be pressed into the thick part of the flesh leaving no impression, the flesh can be considered as cured.

STORAGE Store the fish in wooden boxes lined with wax

paper. Scatter a little dry salt between each layer of fish—about one pound of salt to 10 pounds of fish. Store in as cool and dry a place as possible. If signs of rust or mold appear scrub the fish off in brine and dry in the air for a day or two.

RECIPES FOR PREPARATION OF DRIED FISH

FRESHENING If the fish have not been too heavily salted, freshening in several cold waters over night or from eight to 48 hours, according to the taste, should be sufficient. But should further freshening be needed, par-boil, that is, put on in cold water to cover, and just bring to a boil. Then simmer, as boiling tends to toughen the fish. The process may be completed by any method of cookery suitable for salt fish, such as broiling, frying, baking in milk or cream, simmering, or creaming etc. Usually the fish need more freshening for the first two cookery methods named above than for methods requiring milk or other combinations which tend to mask the excess salty flavor. Running water will hasten the freshening.

SALTED MULLET—BROILED Remove all scales, freshen for eight to 12 hours, drain. Oil the fish on both sides, now the broiler rack, and broil five to six minutes on each side. Season with pepper, then butter and serve hot.

BAKED IN MILK To one pound of fish that has been freshened, use one cup of whole milk, two teaspoons of butter, paprika and white pepper.

Pour the milk over the fish that has been placed skin side down in a pan or iron skillet. Preheat the oven for 10 minutes.

When 450 degrees Fahrenheit, put in the fish and bake until a very small amount of liquid remains. Remove fish to platter, and butter to the liquid and pour over the fish. Dash on paprika.

CREAMED SALTED FLAKES

1 1/2 cups cooked cold fish flakes

2 cups whole milk

4 tablespoons fat

4 tablespoons flour

1/2 teaspoon Worcestershire sauce pepper

Make a cream sauce of the fat, flour, and liquid. When smooth, add the seasoning and blend. Add fish flakes. Heat through. Serve on toast, waffles or in ramekins. Strips of pimento make nice garnish.

BOILED SALT SPANISH MACKEREL Clean and freshen in cold water over night, or longer as necessary. Put fish in a skillet or deep pan, cover with cold water and heat slowly. At least an hour. Do not boil. When it has reached the temperature of boiling, lower the fire and simmer another hour or until it is tender. Skim off scum. Remove to platter and serve with plain boiled buttered potatoes, or with an egg sauce.

Note: While the directions given above are for specific varieties of fish, they will apply generally to most any variety. A little experimenting will develop the cookery to best suit your tastes.

HOME CANNING OF FISH

From Information Distributed by the
U. S. FISH AND WILDLIFE SERVICE

PRESSURE COOKER ESSENTIAL The use of a pressure cooker for processing non-acid meats and vegetables is recommended by most State and Federal agriculture experiment stations and extension services. Recently, however, home-canning bulletins have been published by some manufacturers of glass jars, and by certain other agencies, in which processing in hot water or in an oven are recommended as optional methods. These bulletins contribute to the erroneous belief of many home canners that a satisfactory heat treatment can be obtained by these more or less makeshift methods. It cannot be emphasized too strongly that under no circumstances should any fishery product be canned unless a pressure canner is used. It is impossible to obtain a sufficient heat treatment by any other means.

Fish properly preserved by canning will retain their original color, flavor, and texture much longer than by most other methods, and if stored under reasonable conditions they will remain in excellent condition for several years.

The fundamental principle of canning is the application of

heat to food in hermetically sealed containers and for periods of time sufficient to destroy any yeasts, molds, or enzymes, and to destroy or render inactive any bacterial organisms to cause spoilage. A short treatment at a high temperature, or a long treatment at a lower temperature may destroy these active, vegetative organisms. A temperature sufficient to destroy spoilage organisms establishes the minimum temperature, while quality considerations determine the maximum. Sometimes these limits are close together.

PANS AND KETTLES Pans and kettles in which raw materials are kept, or in which they are pre-cooked or otherwise prepared for canning, should be of a good grade of aluminum or stainless steel. Copper and galvanized-iron kettles and pans are liable to cause discoloration and unpleasant flavors in the finished products.

GLASS JARS Due to difficulties in obtaining "tin" cans, this discussion will be concerned only with packing in glass jars. The jars should not be over one pint in capacity, and the use of half-pint containers is not economical.

The caps should be the self sealing type, fitted with enameled metal tops edged with an inert composition gasket. These are preferred over all other types of lids. Examine the jars carefully for defects.

HANDLING AND TRANSPORTATION Fish should not be left exposed to the full rays of the sun or thrown into the bottom of the boat where they will be stepped upon and bruised. To delay spoilage and improve the color of the flesh, fish should be bled immediately after they are caught. After bleeding, they should be packed in finely crushed ice; or, if crushed ice is not available, theys hould be thoroughly cleaned, the belly cavities rubbed with fine salt, and placed in a ventilated covered box. A piece of burlap, or gunny sack, frequently wetted with water will make an excellent cover, but it should not rest on the fish. The box also may be used for transporting the fish home. Every effort should be made to get the fish home in the best possible condition.

DRESSING AND WASHING Even if the fish were cleaned when caught, they will require further cleaning and washing before canning. At this time the fins must be removed, the fish scraped free from scales and slime, the heads and tails cut off, and any remaining bits of viscera or membranes cleaned from the cavity. After washing in fresh water, the color of the flesh usually can be improved by soaking 15 to 60 minutes in a light brine, made in the proportions of one-half cup of salt to one gallon of water. This drains diffused blood out of the flesh.

PREPARATION FOR THE CONTAINER Salmon, shad, and similar varieties are packed raw with no preparation other than cutting into container length pieces. Others are pre-cooked for a short time before filling into containers. Pre-cooking removes excess moisture, thus making the canned product firmer, makes filling easier, helps to create a vacuum in the container, and eliminates the exhausting step. It also shortens the time required for processing in the cooker as the product is hot when the container is put into the pressure canner. Pre-cooking may also be used to impart a desired flavor or to remove some undesirable natural flavor. Avoid delays in handling at this stage.

VACUUM Products packed in glass need not be put through an exhaust process, as in tin, to obtain a vacuum. Exhaust occurs during processing because the containers are not then completely sealed.

All containers must be cooled as rapidly as possible after processing, otherwise the stored-up heat will continue cooking and the contents will be overcooked. Care must be used in cooling glass. The glass jars must be so stacked that air can pass freely around them, but they should be protected from drafts while cooling. When the jars are practically cool they should be washed and dried.

Inspect all containers carefully for signs of leaking or other defects before storing them. No attempt should be made to reprocess leaky containers of fishery products, even though discovered at once.

RECOMMENDED CANNING METHODS The methods herein given are for products specifically named. While the processes are believed to be adequate for the sterilization of practically all varieties, some species of fish, because of certain physical and chemical properties, are not suited to canning.

Therefore, if it is desired to can a species not similar to those hereafter listed, it will be well to experiment with more than one method, selecting the one that gives best results. For example, firm-fleshed fish that would produce a palatable product if canned by the method given for salmon might be considered much better if packed tuna-style.

The home canner should bear in mind that this bulletin is intended only as a guide' not a series of infallible recipes, and much depends upon the care in following general directions.

MACKEREL, LAKE TROUT, WHITEFISH, AND FLORIDA MULLET:

1. Clean, wash in fresh water and drain a few minutes.

2. Split the fish, leave backbone, cut in container lengths. Soak in brine, made of 1/2 pound salt to one gallon of water for 60 minutes.

3. Drain brined fish and fill into jars, flush. Alternate heads and tails. Skin side against glass. Submerge the open jars in brine, made of four ounces of salt to one gallon of water, and bring to a boil for 15 minutes.

4. Remove jars, invert on wire screen to drain for three minutes. Discard drained liquid. Add one or two bay leaves and one or two slices of onion to each jar.

5. Process in the pressure canner for 100 minutes at 10 pounds pressure (240 degrees). Release pressure very slowly from the pressure canner, allowing 20 minutes or more, and remove jars. At this point the jars are now sealed tightly as glass jars must not be completely sealed before they are processed—the lids are merely laid in place and rings loosely screwed during the processing in the canner.

To fill 12 pint jars, 35 pounds or round weight fish are needed.

CARP AND SUCKERS

1. Clean, remove fins, skin, and streak of dark flesh along each side. Split the fish, leave backbone, cut into container lengths.

2. Wash and soak in brine (1/4 cup of salt to one gallon of water) for 30 minutes. Remove and drain.

3. Rub fish with dry salt and pack in stone crock for two hours with as much salt as will cling to flesh.

4. Rinse fish in fresh water and pack in jars after draining.

5. Place lids on jars loosely and steam for 30 minutes at three pounds pressure (220 degrees Fahrenheit). Remove and invert over a screen to drain for two or three minutes.

6. Place a bay leaf on top of fish and fill up each jar with chopped onion. Glass jars must not be completely sealed before they are processed.

7. Process: Pint jars 100 minutes at 10 pounds pressure (240 degrees Fahrenheit).

TUNA-STYLE PACK This method is best for albacore or white meat tuna, tuna, king mackerel, and mackerel. Only large mackerel should be used

1. After washing, place fish in pans with perforated bottoms and stack these in pressure canner. Cook two hours at one degree (10 pounds).

2. Cool cooked fish several hours then scrape away skin with knife, lift out backbone, and cut away streaks of dark flesh along the sides. Cut meat into sections a little shorter than jars.

3. Put 1/2 teaspoon of salt and three tablespoons of olive oil or cottonseed oil in each empty jar—half pints recommended for this type pack. Fill meat solidly, using small flakes to fill out.

4. Process: seal glass jars loosely and process for 80 minutes at 15 pounds pressure. Remove jars and tighten tops.

   CAUTION: If spoilage is suspected, even in slight degree,

do not attempt to verify the fact by tasting the product. One taste of a spoiled canned fishery product may cause serious illness or death. When opening a jar observe the contents, and if they seem unduly soft or have a cheesy, sour, or tainted odor it is reasonable to suspect spoilage. Spoiled products should be destroyed at once, preferably by burning.

MAKE A CARDBOARD
SMOKEHOUSE

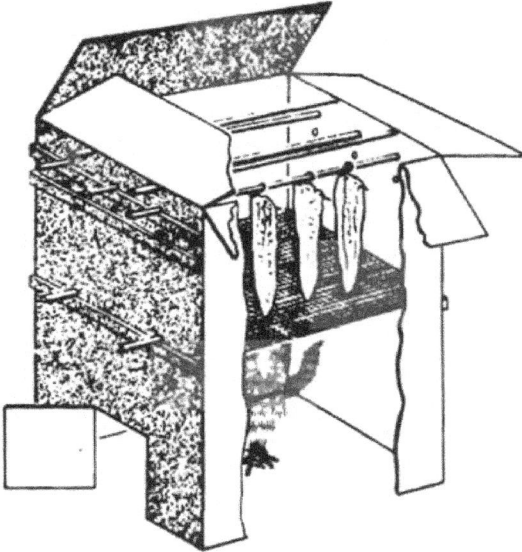

As further evidence that you do not have to have anything so very fancy to get into fish smoking, here is a design for a cardboard smoke house. Not that we suggest this as the best method, but if you are crowded for time and don't have easy access to the materials needed for the more permanent smoke houses then the cardboard job can serve the purpose and may whet your desire to make an even better rig. Believe us, it really works and has the extra advantage of being completely portable.

Actually all you need is any enclosure that will hold the smoke. In the sketch above the box is 30 inches square and 48 inches high. The least you can get by with is 24 inches in width or depth and 40 inches high.

It is a good idea to reinforce the cardboard box by tacking on wood strips at the corners—use large head roofing nails that won't pull through. Horizontal pieces tacked on about four inches from top and bottom will give you a fairly sturdy rig. Use any appropriate cross rods to hold the fish and reinforce the holes, if necessary, by tacking a strip underneath the holes, as shown. A piece of hardware cloth rests on a couple of cross rods to catch any fish that may come off the hooks. The door, for attending the fire, is made by two cuts on the cardboard—10 inches wide, 12 inches high. The bottom of the box remains open by pushing the flaps in and the top remains closed after the fish are hung on the rods.

One more note on construction:—if you can't get one big box, it is possible to telescope together two smaller boxes of the same size. Where the boxes join, remove the flaps and by carefully compressing the inside box at the corners the two can be pushed together. Tie string around the whole job to keep the corners from breaking out.

To keep some circulation of air and smoke, cut a one inch square "U" shaped flap on the back near the top—this will permit some smoke to escape and any other escapement around the holes and joints is ok.

Pre-treatment of the fish, salting, drying, the use of hooks, and selection of the right wood etc. are the same as described earlier in this book.

OPERATION

From 5 to 6 hours are required to smoke the fish ready to eat, the exact period depending upon the size of the fish. The carton will not catch fire if the ventilation is controlled and the fire is suffocated to smoke and not blaze. Should too large a blaze develop—smother it with sawdust or remove the blazing wood. Use semi-dry non-resinous woods such as oak, hickory, beech, and sweet bay and for extra flavor add one or more of the following: river mangrove, palmetto roots, apple wood, citrus or leeched drift wood. Corn cobs, coconut husks, sawdust and chips of the above are good. Sawdust burns slowly and makes a good smudge, however, too heavy a smoke over-emphasizes the smoke flavor. Never use the pines or pitchy woods. The idea is to prepare the fire first then place the box with the fish in it over the fire. Allow your fire to get going well enough so that when it is smothered over it will have enough heat of its embers to keep up a steady smoke.

After placing the box over the fire, push dirt around the

bottom of the box. Do not have the door on the lee side. Place any handy object on top of the box to hold the flaps together.

The fire should be tended every half hour. For the first 4 or 5 hours the temperature should be held to around 100°F or below, then increased between 180° to 200°F for about an hour. The progress of the smoking can be observed by lifting the top flaps—take a look at about 2 1/2 hours and thereafter every half hour. The cooking is complete when the backbone of the fish separates from the meat. To keep insects away from the fish while they are cooling you can cover with mosquito netting. This is the Hot Smoke Method—it imparts a most delicious flavor and leaves the texture succulent.

TROT LINE FISHING

Another good Netcraft "How to do it" booklet

There is plenty of fun and adventure in trot line fishing. It combines an overnight outing with a nice fire under a summer sky with the thrill of "running the line" and feeling the tugs and jerks that telegraph that there is a good one on at the hook station you are about to attend. And the size of some of these "cats"—you should see the pictures and the unique baits and methods used to catch 'em. All the inside secrets are here with plenty of good drawings that show you every step of the way: How to make up a trot line, How to prepare tie the staging, and various methods of attaching to the main line. You'll also learn how to bait the line—tricks in setting it for river and lake. Here is a wealth of grand information——Price 50c. Published by The Netcraft Company, Toledo 13, Ohio.

www.ingramcontent.com/pod-product-compliance
Lightning Source LLC
Chambersburg PA
CBHW031007090426
42737CB00008B/720